SCARRED CANVAS
selected poems

by
RC EDRINGTON

Published by Underground Voices

ISBN: 978-0-9830456-4-9

Printed in the United States of America.

©2012 RC Edrington

"I'm all the time aware it's reality and not literature I'm engaged in."
-Alexander Trocchi

"Whom the gods notice they destroy. Be small...and you will escape the jealousy of the great." -Philip K. Dick

Some of these poems appeared previously in:

*Underground Voices, Zygote In My Coffee
Impetus, Bone Orchard Poetry
Polluto UK, Blue Chrome Press UK
Pipe Dream, Ten Page Press
Unlikely Stories, Red Fez*

Dedicated to those I somehow lost along the way. I miss you all dearly.

CONTENTS

Dumb Ass Artist	pg. 7
for Cait	pg. 9
Melissa Sometimes	pg. 11
As She Sleeps	pg. 12
Cigarette Moment	pg. 13
For Lack of Bullets	pg. 15
Ghosts of Hollywood	pg. 17
Used Furniture	pg. 19
Bridgette	pg. 21
Spent Angel Blues	pg. 23
Ritual de lo Habitual	pg. 25
Vacant	pg. 27
Tattooed Beat Messiah	pg. 28
Junkie Love	pg. 31
Still In Hollywood	pg. 33
Unbroken	pg. 35
Scarred & Twisted	pg. 37
Sick Fucks	pg. 40
Black Convertible Jaguar Chrome	pg. 42
Another Drunk Poem	pg. 44
Stay	pg. 47
7 a.m.	pg. 48
Lipstick Bruise	pg. 50
Pretty Little Mess	pg. 51
Scarred Canvas	pg. 54
for Riki	pg. 56
Dope	pg. 59
Lines Between the Fix	pg. 60

Dumb Ass Artist

your typical cliche
wanna-be hip artist
draped in black
always hung outside
the right circles
sipped wine
from Styrofoam cups
at all the gallery
openings downtown
chain smoked
my cigarettes
gave up discussing art
when I told him
I only came to get laid
& none of these fucks
would ever paint their way
out of a bad marriage
told me when he
checked out
he had a 2' x 4' white
gesso primed canvas
to lean like a mini
emergency room stretcher
against the shower stall
had the right distance
marked off
so when he pulled
the trigger
only his blood & brains
would hit the canvas
& not the shotgun blast
told me I could sell
his suicide
to any gallery

that now rejected him
if I promised
to drink a toast
to his memory
the night they found
the dumb ass
OD'd on Mexican Tar
in the parking lot
behind the Buffet Bar
I honestly tried
to feign disappointment

Scarred Canvas

for Cait

she encouraged me
my art was in language
not subject,
so all the bloodstains
& dull syringes
from all the nubile
junkie whores
& quick amphetamine
sex & diseases
scattered thru
my words & syntax
like tarnished pennies
around crisp dollar bills
in that battered guitar case
tossed like a spent body
on that 4th avenue sidewalk
where I used to scream
the blues
held a value & truth
all their own,
so I scribbled what I knew
& she published
what I knew,
but damn I miss her badly
& she taught me enough
to know
her epitaph belongs
in one of my jaded,
self absorbed pieces
no more than it did
in the obituaries that day
when my eyes exploded
with tears,

Scarred Canvas

like an infected vein
shooting pus & blood
against a graffiti scarred
bus depot
bathroom mirror

Scarred Canvas

Melissa Sometimes

saxophone squeals
broken notes to heartache,
Leonard Cohen croons
through this paper thin
hotel wall

down in the alley
wanna be jive-boy white punks
dance to a desperate beat
called gang-bang,
cop $10 bills from worn
teenage Latino whores

& snowflakes gather
along this frozen window sill
like an Albino's dry leper skin,
as my syringe slowly soaks
up the final spilt tear
of a pawned diamond ring

& I still think of you
Melissa sometimes
do you still think of me,
are you somewhere
swaying to Coltrane
blackberry Merlot raping
your carved Cherokee cheeks

& when the phone rings
at desperate 3 a.m.
to only voiceless,
dead air
do you sometimes wish
or know it was me?

As She Sleeps

Words that touch me
in ways lips,
fingers never will.

Her voice
a caress
that dimples the skin
taught upon my soul.

I want to listen
hour upon hour,
& often do...
while she lays asleep,
while my cigarette burns,
when the whiskey fails
to carry me
to a shelter that exists
only in her arms.

Cigarette Moment

*"I don't remember lighting this cigarette
and I don't remember if I'm here alone
or waiting for someone."* -Leonard Cohen

I need
a cigarette
& a stiff
double splash
on ice.
Gin with a lemon
curve of breast.

I need
your nude body
to slip
from my mind
like fingers
lost between thighs.

I need this ache
for you
to wake alone
& drunk at 5 a.m.
without a name.

I need a drink.
Gin with a lemon
curve of lips.

Scarred Canvas

I need
your memory
to fade
from this room
like wisps of smoke
from this
stale cigarette.

For Lack Of Bullets

Johnny Walker Red
bottle lay empty
& too bad
the .357 that lurks
beneath this cigarette
scarred mattress
does too

tonight death
tongues my ear
like a sickly whore
in need of that final fix,
one more taste
to course the veins

& I offer
no more poetical devices,

no more lame attempts
to purge some fresh
hip language
from this rotten core

& this is not
a poem,

this is a worn syringe
tossed into
the moldy haystack
of drunken macho man
literature

Scarred Canvas

this is last call
in a Mexican cantina
where marijuana
& cigar smoke
stifle the air
like cheap perfume
that drowns a toothless
$10 whore
who sits with one eye
cocked in boredom
as I finger my change
for a Mexican taxi

each blackened peso
a memory romanticized
through a thin veil
of alcohol,
dope & time

...a time when
the world was a flirt
that shivered my senses
in slutty whispers,
& none of my lovers
gorged the last
blood drop
from my sun-chapped soul,
as they lay overdosed
on a stainless steel slab
like a freshly hooked trout,
waiting to be gutted...

Ghosts of Hollywood

sirens echo screams
through this dingy hotel wall

seems we all have animals
we must cage...
dragons we must chase

I close my eyes
or do my eyes close me
as heroin tongues sweet laps
through my bloodstream

I fuck the ghosts
of Hollywood starlets
on cotton swab clouds

while down in the alley
Judy Garland leans
her anorexic
junkie shoulders
against a piss stained
red brick wall

hikes her pink silk sleeve
to reveal powder
baby blue veins
that scar her arm
of alabaster marble

& tonight Judy & I
are not afraid

Scarred Canvas

to die
would be like sticking
our souls
instead of
simply our tongues
between midnights
bruised thighs

as we drift
like ghosts
into the silhouette
of this moment

Used Furniture

Bridgette used to be
a model, but then
even I
used to be
something...

like used furniture
that has lost its shape
& style,
we rot away the days
collecting dust
in this roach infected
hotel room

to numb the days
that drip slowly
like rusty rain
from this cracked
plaster ceiling
Bridgette nods
through a heroin daze

as I try to rescue
my fiery teenage soul
lost between the words
that form these worn
middle-aged lines

but like a junkie
rifling beneath
torn cushions
of a broken down couch,
for a few quarters
to cop the next fix

Scarred Canvas

my fingers fill
with absence,
like a faded ghost
clinging to
a brittle corsage

trapped between
the yellowed pages
of a high school
yearbook

Bridgette

late nite nicotine
jet black coffee
fueled by
shots of Jim Beam

worn radio plays
the way worn radios
always seem to play
static & soft cool jazz
tinged by solo sobs
of a pawned saxophone
in this stale & musty
hotel room

& there is nothing
on my mind
as cigarette smoke
curls & drifts
like some wayward ghost
out this open window
& down into
the un-lit alley

where somewhere lost
amidst the dumpsters
amidst the piss & puke
soaked cardboard boxes

amidst the spent
wine bottles
cracked & bleeding
on the trash scarred
asphalt like
the homeless flesh

that once nursed them
into emptiness

there is a rose
straining its way up
thru the torn membrane
of a patch of soil
in ache of dawn

& I only need
to close my dry,
bloodshot eyes
& listen in faith
to know it's there

a faith I once wasted
on you

Scarred Canvas

Spent Angel Blues
"Selling my soul would be a lot easier if I could just find it." -Nikki Sixx

In this room of things which strain to move
time lies overdosed on the cold cement
bathroom floor.
There are no cigarettes left
to ease its passing.
No songs remain
to fill the empty spaces
where once drifted the subtle strokes
of its blood beat.

There is only stillness,
a tea spoon
of Black Tar heroin
& memories...

At 29
my friends are dead
strung-out, jailed, or
trapped in between
the cynical Styrofoam walls
of mental institutions
like freshly hooked trout
in an ice chest
waiting to be gutted.

They've left me here, alone
to only the stale glow
of a blinking neon sign
in which to perfect this dying art,
to write anarchistic odes to our youth
shattered like a glass syringe
against a red bricked schoolyard wall...

Scarred Canvas

but tonight
the memory of Traci haunts me.
The night they found her naked
blood caked body
tossed away like a cum stained Kleenex
right on the sidewalk
in front of 100 screaming tourists
who till this day don't believe
the pretty bright lights of Hollywood
are fueled by the charred mounds
of runaway teenage flesh
searching to fulfill childhood dreams
but only end up filling their fragile orifices
with whatever perverted disease
the man with the $20 bill wants...

So I continue to walk
this death row promenade of memories,
perhaps the way
a sergeant walks a post war graveyard
wondering if all these bodies
should somehow add up to something more
than a few medals for his chest...
or a few lines in my notebook.

& as the heroin begins to burn
like napalm through my veins
blood rises in the thin syringe
like a scarlet mushroom cloud
over Hollywood Blvd.
& for the spent angels of the apocalypse
another personal Armageddon
draws temporarily...
always so fucking temporarily
to a close.

Ritual de lo Habitual

we duct taped
faded newspapers
to the bedroom windows
to erase the sun

silence between us
palpable & black
like fresh tar
on a once familiar road
we would never wander
together again...

a long ignored
cigarette
burnt itself out
on a crushed
Diet Pepsi can,
ash bent & ready to fall
like a timid suicide
perched upon
the Golden Gate Bridge

time itself
a false restraint
we somehow escaped
as we sat like
twin Buddha's rotting
on a flesh smeared
mattress

each moment
you held me
tight in your soft heroin

gauzed sleep,
I knew you dreamed
of someone else...
as did I

both too weak
to break old habits
& embrace the slit of dawn
that crept slow beneath
the fist battered
bedroom door

Vacant

*"We're so pretty, oh so pretty...
pretty vacant." -Sex Pistols*

There's nothing more empty
than a refrigerator w/o a door
except for the windowless room
where it lays on its side
three feet away from a naked girl
sobbing on a cement floor
in the frail arms of a man who
would steal her last $10 bill
if she had one
& she knows it
because to him there's nothing
more empty than a syringe
staring from top the refrigerator
except for his blurred eyes
which are my eyes
& can no longer focus
the carved features
of a boyish face
shattered in a mirror
with a fist & left bleeding
beside an unplugged refrigerator
& down the naked back
of a girl whose soul
has become
just another hole
aching to be filled

Tattooed Beat Messiah
for Amy

She sucks a Marlboro
then huffs the smoke
thru her flared nostrils,
reminding me
of the tattooed basilisk
guarding her left breast.

Pretends to be reading
when she's only
flipping thru the pages
of "*On the Road*".

I toss back another
shot of Cuervo Gold,
then suck a lemon wishing
we were making love
instead of arguing
on this porch,

while she straddles the rail
& flirts with the clouds.

She places the beat bible
on the rail
then grinds out
her cigarette into the cover,
as tho it were my arm.

Scarred Canvas

Another shot of tequila
& I'd be out
the back gate & into
the alley stumbling...
probably end up sleeping alone
in someone's rented car,

so I toss the bottle
out into the yard
& wonder
what the clouds see
in her.

It has to be her red hair.
The way the sun sets it ablaze
with the reckless abandon
of children dabbling
in matches.

Or her pink leather pants,
how they cling to her curves
like the soft smooth palms
of a sculptor to his Venus.

She lights another Marlboro
wishing she were shooting-up
or at least stoned,
& nearly falls off the rail
as I shout:

"Look, I'll have no poem
of mine tattooed
on your or anyone's ass..."
realizing

Scarred Canvas

I probably never again
get to tongue
the angels
trumpeting open
the gates of heaven
tattooed below
her naval.

Junkie Love

How can you be so shocked, Katrina?
The only things we truly shared
in this 6 month cliche
of "homie-lover-friend" barrio affair

where we isolated ourselves
& nearly rotted away
like 2 lost, alien crash babies
on that blood, shit, piss, & cum
tapestry of mattress
tossed like another wasted
& useless sack of flesh
in that water logged corner
bedroom in Joe's abandoned house,
were a few top notch
fucks & sucks...
a few dull & dirty syringes...
& about 8-10 ounces
of that cheap sugar-cut
Mexican tar.

So come on Katrina,
when the dope ran out,
and so did I...
I may not have returned
with prison green
tattooed arms
draped in roses,
or those 2 silver & turquoise
bear claw engagement rings
you spoke circles
and circles about...

Scarred Canvas

But fuck Katrina,
I didn't leave you with Hep C
Or HIV either...

Still In Hollywood

*"And so it's 3 a.m., I'm out walking again.
I'm just a spot on the sidewalk in a city of sin."* -Johnette Napolitano

We spoke,
not remembering our lines
so well rehearsed.
For a moment,
we shed our masks
like soldiers after a war.
I pulled the mirrored lenses from my eyes,
hung my cracked & dusty leather
on a rusty nail & held you
for the first time,
in a long time
with my own skin
pressed firmly against yours.

Words wafting from your lips
like the sweet, sweet smell
of marijuana seeping
from beneath the backstage door.

The relief of holding you again.
I'm sorry I left,
but is that enough?

The scars across my heart
like the tattoos on my arms,
still remain.

A decade of playing cool.
Days running into days into years.
The caved veins of punk romance.
The midnight amphetamine tremors
that left me stumbling

Scarred Canvas

thru a corridor of mirrors,
reaching out to find myself
but only finding
the cold hospital steel of polished glass.
Too cool. Too smooth.

Slam dancing in pneumonia infected dives
to the thunderous crash of un-tuned guitars,
as the blood of friends-strangers-enemies
(god does it matter anymore?)
slowly caked around
the studded spikes I wore so proud.

But here we are again,
if only for one sacred moment,
sobered by the death of a friend
who placed her soul into a syringe
& left it trembling
on Hollywood Blvd.

I'd thank god it wasn't you,
if I could find one...
walking alone down this suicide stained street
who didn't believe salvation
could be bought or sold in plastic bags.

Unbroken

If I had a dime
for every dish daddy
splattered like a
defective clay pigeon
into the kitchen wall
& a dollar for
every bruise
that eclipsed mamma's
sad blue eyes like
some dark, dying star
& maybe a nickel
here & there
for every childhood
bone splintered like
a rotted bamboo shoot
in dad's drunken
Vietnam enraged hands

I'd be a millionaire
getting my cock honed
by 18 year old
coke whores in some
ghost tainted mansion
on that Beverly Hill
where loyalty is metered
by the powdery white
prison bars that cut
a mirror no one ever
bothers to gaze
too deeply into
& not this
semi-reformed
heroin fiend laying
next to you, Marie

Scarred Canvas

biding my time
between your breasts
& the steady
blood rhythm
of your heartbeat
with a notebook full
of paper promises,
IOU's for love
drawn on the failed
bank of poetry

waiting,
sweet Marie...
always waiting
for your lips to find me
in this wide expanse
of dream
where like a wild Mustang
I buck free
of dad's reins

Scarred & Twisted
for Carol

bedroom door
locked tight to erase
moonlights sole witness

18 we are not
anymore...

green eyes soft & shut
hair red & fluff-ed
against cream satin pillow,
dreams tucked closely
like knees
against her chin

slowly
she fingers
her freshly powdered breasts
scented with mom's
most expensive
top shelf perfume

as cheap vodka slowly
breaths & swirls thru the air

it is here
& here only
for a moment brief
she is not ashamed
of things she touches,

the memories she tongues
to life against my ear,

Scarred Canvas

in lights blackened
behind sealed doors
where friends & colleagues
boyfriends & real life lovers
are not around
to pass cigarettes,
puffs of time...
& judgment

it is only this
ghost of who I am
& her desire of me
that shames her most

both enlightened
by yesterday,
age & time...

I, a bad 2 minute punk song
screamed from a chaotic
beer stained stage,
my soul scarred & twisted
by 20 years of a world
deformed by factory,

a myth
that never took root,

a figure she
once glimpsed
in some art house movie

both of us unable
to now recall...

Scarred Canvas

she
quite unaware
this darkness she requires
me to exist & linger in
will soon
suck us both
so much deeper into
the nothingness
from which we crawled

so drunk
so disorderly

I back to my corner pub
begging for change
as I cut 8 ball
with cue ball

her
back to
the over priced shrinks
with their pills of many colors
as she tries
ever so hard
to just be
daddy's sweet little
rich girl
one more time

Sick Fucks

in a trailer
with boarded-up windows
on 33rd & 5th
a rookie cop puked
into a shit clogged toilet
& called for an ambulance
despite the fact
2 year old Melissa
had been rotting
from starvation
& dehydration
for at least a week
while in the trash
cluttered bedroom
momma lay overdosed
with a welfare check
coursing pure Afghani
heroin through her caved
hypodermic veins

2 blocks away
on South 6th Avenue
Johnny's 3rd grade head
bounced like an 8-ball
against a scarred
black hardwood floor
blood splattering
an abstract painting
to stain the vomit
stenched Ice-T shirt
of momma's white-nigger
wanna-be pimp
whacked out on
crack cocaine

Scarred Canvas

3 blocks south
& 1 block east
this alcoholic, junkie writer
sits at a pool hall
& slams his
5th shot of Jose Cuervo
& fist against the bar
while Shorty passes
a Folgers coffee can
for the families
left behind
& tells me services
will be held at
St. Augustine's Cathedral
over on Stone
3 days apart

& in my reflective
drunkeness
I wonder if
these loyal Catholics
had been permitted
condoms & abortion
none of this shit
would have ever had
to go down

Black Convertible Jaguar Chrome

She curtsies up to the curb
draped in black convertible
Jaguar chrome.

Like a stripper fingering g-string,
she peels Ray-Bans from her eyes.

"Need a ride?"

At 45,
cocaine boosts her up
& Xanax slides her down.

Says, "My husband fondles
stock-tables, stewardesses & waitresses
but back at home,
his bank account
& blood pressure
are the only things that ever rise."

Black leather sofa.
Diamond earrings.
Our gin & tonic tongues exchange
ice cubes, a curve of lime.

Her red fingernails disappear
between her sad middle-aged thighs
like the tail-lights on her Jaguar
slipping around
an un-lit Beverly Hill road.

Scarred Canvas

She stuffs $20's like fingers
into the front pocket
of my ripped & faded jeans,
then sips cigarette.

Her brake-lights pause,
then wink goodbye.

In snakeskin boots I slither
down sidewalk
in search of pawned guitar.

She said, "When you write of me...
& promise you will write of me,
make me younger.
I was so much more beautiful
when I was young like you."

Another Drunk Poem

tired of poems
full of cocks & cunts
dripping their herpes
& yeast infections
across the white
dying lips of art

pissed off at
posers & voyeurs
who form gods out of boozer's,
& kneel on their Bukowski books
to peek thru keyholes
that ooze with blood & vomit
& the kind of life
their daddy can't buy
with American Express
or implied

I have no desire
to continue
typing & writing
writing & typing
to pick open scabs
on my heart & knees

to peel off this bandage
of black leather jacket
to flash my tracks
or prison green tattoos
or tell how many chicks
I did or didn't fuck
in that punk bar
soon to be spraying orgasm
in a peep show near you

Scarred Canvas

tired & pissed & drunk
deep in the wallow
of alleged friends
who claim I've sold out
yet I remind them
the sole difference
between this bullshit
they call poetry
& the whore on 6th avenue
who flashes her tits & ass
at trolling cars
is she gets paid

right now I'll settle for
a bottle of single malt scotch
& 24 hours of MTV
to numb my senses
on this popular
throw away culture

want to scribble odes
to orgasmic flowers
& bottled water
want to write love sonnets
to women who never leave me

puking in a sink
or passed out in a driveway

want to write romantic stuff
just like all of you
pencil pushing clones
& leave out all this shit
about whiskey, dope & bars

Scarred Canvas

but I feel I'm gonna puke again
feel I'm gonna shoot-up again
feel I'm gonna fuck
& fall out of love again

so have your video cameras cued

Stay

in absence
of my chest ablaze
in a fiery tangle
of her teased red hair,
she sleepily exhales
a kaleidoscope of dreams
& promises left
unfulfilled

while this drunken hero
splashes cheap brandy
into a paper cup,
inhales the butt of night
for its last hit of smoke,
then grinds it to ash
into the bedpost

I know she must leave,
but must she leave
the sweat & musk
of my spent body
to linger like the scent
of some exotic douche
between her thighs

as she slips into
her panties
& rushes home
to a husband
who has left empty
even more of her dreams
than I?

7 a.m.

she cuddles nude
in a puddle of pillows
on the studio floor
as tho she's always
belonged here

while I sit
at this knife scarred
kitchen table
& choke down
stale bits of bagel
between shots
of Jack Daniels

last night
she wanted love

I just wanted
to lose myself
inside the ache
of her pale
tattooed skin

this morning
I sit & stare
at her pale legs
& breasts
waiting
for her to arise

Scarred Canvas

& decide if
she still will need
what I hope
she doesn't think
either of us
may have truly found

Lipstick Bruise

Alone in 3 a.m.
bus depot silence,
whiskey bottle lingers
on my lips & tongue
like a kiss I once tasted,
& now refuses to drift
from my memory.

Perhaps she touched me
in places
I never wanted her
to touch, places
no one's touched before.

I expecting only
a one night "I'm leaving
Los Angeles tomorrow" affair.

I never wanting
of her lips
against my waking chest
to only dream.

Lips that tonight
call out to me.

Lips like fingertips.
Fingertips that sting my skin
Like fresh tattoos.

Pretty Little Mess

you gothic waif
with your "oh so sad" cliche
of smudged black mascara
& charcoal blackened lips,

polished red leather
mini-skirt & bra shining
like cheap blow-up doll latex
in this forced & tamed
Hollywood terrace moonlight...

You know
I'll write the books
about your lonely 3 a.m.
nosebleeds, Kleenex
tossed like Tampons
in your kitchen trash
& that antique Betty Boop
cigarette case,

chalk white
with that baby laxative
cut cocaine
you hide beneath
your microwave.

so roll your vacant
23 yr old mall rat eyes
at my tired life
at my barrio whores & junkies
at my low rent criminal friends

Scarred Canvas

all you truly desire
my Prozac numbed
wrist slitting Juliet
is to capture me
in this deluxe 3 bedroom
condo cage toy box

as tho I am some lost
& hopeless romantic poster child
for punk rock tortured artist

but an artist I am not,
despite how much
of your dead dad's cash
you stuff like sluttish fingers
into the front pockets
of my frayed jeans
crumpled like
an old love letter
on your bedroom floor,

as I sleep to dream
of somewhere
& someone else

I am exactly who
& what I am,
nothing more
nothing less,
but sometimes

when I am buried deep
inside of you,
my eyes clenched shut
against that stupid
pentagram tattoo stain

Scarred Canvas

stabbed between
your tender shoulder blades,

I wonder who
& what exactly
you think you are...

Scarred Canvas

Like a lost car
from a funeral promenade
she drifts ghostly
along the snow-lit shop fronts,
with the collar of her
long black trench coat
cocked like a vulture wing
against her pale neck
& cheekbones.

As she tosses her golden hair
against the winter frost,
wheat fields in Kansas sway.

But she does not smile.
She is tired of men
who liken her hair
to wheat fields,
who claim to see mermaids
puddling in the powder blue
pools of her eyes.

She does not smile.
She does not want me
to call her teeth pearls
then pluck them away
while she sleeps.

Pausing, she stares
through her reflection
on a gallery window,
& into a fresh stained canvas
as though it were
the familiar face

Scarred Canvas

of someone
she once may have loved.

A face which pulls her
into a world
draped in red & purple hues
on nights she feels like
shades of gray.

A world where she almost...
but she does not smile.

& as she raises
her frail bird-boned hands
to wipe fresh teardrops
from her eyes,
she reveals thin scars
carved up & down
her pale wrist.

Then she slowly fades
into the un-lit alley way...
fades like a much too perfect rose
in the violent hands
of a narcissistic artist,
brushed away by falling snow.

for Riki

outside
the rain gray
like a memory
forgot

keys rattle
like the bones
of dead cops
against the
door knob

inside
a Jim Beam bottle
she neatly
tucked me into
this morning

before she
blew a kiss
then left

I am sheltered
from the playful
flick of her long
horse tail hair
wet & black
like the eyeliner
that drips
down her cold
blushed cheeks

the downtown bus
diesels off
in a smelly

thick fog
of stale
beer farts

she smiles
peels off
her soaked
faded jean skirt
& pink
Betty Boop
t-shirt

tosses them
like a limp
carcass over
the bedroom door

then lays across
the unmade bed
in a mock Jesus
as I slide off
her red high-heels
& white fishnet
stockings
to massage
her tired toes

my fingers
slowly drift
up her thighs
as she kisses
my ear
& whispers
'I missed you'

Scarred Canvas

instead
of a reminder
that once again
I failed
to make it
out of bed

& pick her up
from her
waitress gig
that pays
our bills

Scarred Canvas

Dope

When I look into your eyes all I can see is a soulless silhouette of a person who found happiness in being a pincushion." — Michael Kloss

Jen's a still life
on the sofa
with her snake skin skirt
brushed up to reveal
the tongue like wetness
of her pink silk panties,
& her Judy Garland face
lays half submerged
in a syrupy red puddle
of her new leather jacket,
& if it wasn't for her eyes
adrift in the liquid sky
I just might accuse her
of actually being alive,
but now it's my turn to turn
& as the heroin begins to burn
I can bear witness to nothing
but the water
that rusts snake-like
down this chipped
& cracked
porcelain sink

Lines Between The Fix

*"I'm here to give you my heart
And you want some fashion show"* - Jim Carroll

today's poets
are self-centered
no talent hacks
who believe
they're the next
Bukowski, Ginsberg,
or Whitman
when in reality
they're nothing
but common house flies
sucking the sugary sinews
of a dead corpse

the pabulum they puke up
even more meaningless
then the corpse
from which they fed

I lack the time
desire & energy
to be the next anybody

I barely have time
to scribble
these meaningless words
before it's time
to hustle up
the next $20
& feed this curse
that haunts my veins

Scarred Canvas

to erase all senses
so even you
no talent hacks
cease to exist

RC EDRINGTON BIO

RC Edrington has been a scourge on the small press for years. He's published numerous chapbooks, the first being *Whiskey Coma Blues*. His scribbles have also appeared in countless journals, anthologies, e-zines and magazines. He offers no graduate degree in any imaginary art form. Nor can he produce a certificate of authentication from any hip writing guild to prove he is an actual writer. He despises hip coffee boutiques and the meaningless flesh that haunts them.

Books
Use Once & Destroy Bluechrome Publishing (2005)
Portraits From A Barrio Toilet Stall Blind Leper Press (2007)
Apocalypse Generation Tainted Coffee Press (2010)

Chapbooks
Whiskey Coma Blues by Implosion Press (1991)
Nicotine Dreams (2002)
Lipstick Bruise (2002)
Vacant (2003)
Fleshwounds Ten Page Press (2011)

Scarred Canvas

Scarred Canvas